Explore the Bible ®

Let the Word dwell in you.

Dewey decimal classification: 226.6
Subject headings: CHURCH / EVANGELISTIC WORK / BIBLE. N.T. ACTS—STUDY

ERIC GEIGER
Vice President, LifeWay Resources

MICHAEL KELLY
Director, Groups Ministry

VANCE H. PITMAN
General Editor

JEREMY MAXFIELD
Content Editor

With *Explore the Bible*, groups can expect to engage Scripture in its proper context and be better prepared to live it out in their own context. These book-by-book studies will help participants—

> grow in their love for Scripture;

> gain new knowledge about what the Bible teaches;

> develop biblical disciplines;

> internalize the Word in a way that transforms their lives.

Send questions/comments to: Content Editor, *Explore the Bible: Small-Group Study;* One LifeWay Plaza; Nashville, TN 37234-0152.

Printed in the United States of America

For ordering or inquiries visit *lifeway.com;* write to LifeWay Small Groups; One LifeWay Plaza; Nashville, TN 37234-0152; or call toll free 800-458-2772.

We believe that the Bible has God for its author; salvation for its end; and truth, without any mixture of error, for its matter and that all Scripture is totally true and trustworthy. To review LifeWay's doctrinal guideline, please visit *lifeway.com/doctrinalguideline.*

Scripture quotations are taken from the Holman Christian Standard Bible®, Copyright © 1999, 2000, 2002, 2003, 2009 by Holman Bible Publishers®. Used by permission. Holman Christian Standard Bible®, Holman CSB®, and HCSB® are federally registered trademarks of Holman Bible Publishers.

Session 1 quotation: Oswald J. Smith, *goodreads* [online, cited 5 November 2015]. Available from the Internet: *www.goodreads.com.* Session 2 quotation: Hudson Taylor, *goodreads* [online, cited 5 November 2015]. Available from the Internet: *www.goodreads. com.* Session 3 quotation: Vance H. Pitman, "Send Conference Live Blog: Session 3," *Send Network* [online], 4 August 2015 [cited 5 November 2015]. Available from the Internet: *http://sendnetwork.com.* Session 4 quotation: David Livingstone, *beliefnet* [online, cited 5 November 2015]. Available from the Internet: www. beliefnet.com. Session 5 quotation: Carl F. H. Henry, *goodreads* [online, cited 5 November 2015]. Available from the Internet: *www.goodreads.com.* Session 6 quotation: Nina Gunter, *goodreads* [online, cited 5 November 2015]. Available from the Internet: *www.goodreads.com.*

Connect

 @ExploreTheBible

 facebook.com/ExploreTheBible

 lifeway.com/ExploreTheBible

 ministrygrid.com/web/ExploreTheBible

❯ ABOUT THIS STUDY

GOD IS ON THE MOVE, INVITING AND EMPOWERING YOU TO JOIN HIS GREAT MISSION.

The Bible isn't just a story of what happened thousands of years ago; it's an invitation to join what God has been doing since the beginning of history. As a Christian and as a part of the church, you play a key role in telling others the good news of Jesus. The same God you read about in the Bible is with you right now and is ready to work through you for His amazing purpose.

The Book of Acts provides a dramatic narrative of the continuing work and witness of the risen Lord Jesus through His followers. It's the foundational account of various people, places, and events involved in the birth and growth of the early church. More important, it magnifies the powerful work of the Holy Spirit in propelling the spread of the gospel message to the ends of the earth.

Explore the Bible: Acts, Chapters 1–12 inspires readers with the fact that over and over again, God works through ordinary people—empowered by the Holy Spirit—to accomplish His eternal mission. Believers in the 21st century are now a part of this amazing story.

The *Explore the Bible* series will help you know and apply the encouraging and empowering truth of God's Word. Each session is organized in the following way.

UNDERSTAND THE CONTEXT: This page explains the original context of each passage and begins relating the primary themes to your life today.

EXPLORE THE TEXT: These pages walk you through Scripture, providing helpful commentary and encouraging thoughtful interaction with God through His Word.

OBEY THE TEXT: This page helps you apply the truths you've explored. It's not enough to know what the Bible says. God's Word has the power to change your life.

LEADER GUIDE: This final section provides optional discussion starters and suggested questions to help anyone lead a group in reviewing each section of the personal study.

For helps on how to use *Explore the Bible*, tips on how to better lead groups, or additional ideas for leading, visit: **www.ministrygrid.com/web/ExploreTheBible.**

❯ GROUP COMMITMENT

As you begin this study, it's important that everyone agrees to key group values. Clearly establishing the purpose of your time together will foster healthy expectations and help ease any uncertainties. The goal is to ensure that everyone has a positive experience leading to spiritual growth and true community. Initial each value as you discuss the following with your group.

❏ PRIORITY

Life is busy, but we value this time with one another and with God's Word. We choose to make being together a priority.

❏ PARTICIPATION

We're a group. Everyone is encouraged to participate. No one dominates.

❏ RESPECT

Everyone is given the right to his or her own opinions. All questions are encouraged and respected.

❏ TRUST

Each person humbly seeks truth through time in prayer and in the Bible. We trust God as the loving authority in our lives.

❏ CONFIDENTIALITY

Anything said in our meetings is never repeated outside the group without the permission of everyone involved. This commitment is vital in creating an environment of trust and openness.

❏ SUPPORT

Everyone can count on anyone in this group. Permission is given to call on one another at any time, especially in times of crisis. The group provides care for every member.

❏ ACCOUNTABILITY

We agree to let the members of our group hold us accountable to commitments we make in the loving ways we decide on. Questions are always welcome. Unsolicited advice, however, isn't permitted.

_____   _____

I agree to all the commitments.   Date

❯ GENERAL EDITOR

Vance H. Pitman is the senior pastor of Hope Church in Las Vegas, Nevada. He also serves with the North American Mission Board as a national mobilizer, engaging and mobilizing pastors to plant more churches.

You can follow Vance on Twitter at *@vancepitman*.

› CONTENTS

Session 1   Jesus Gives the Mission *(Acts 1:1-11)* 6

Session 2   The Church Is Born *(Acts 2:1-4,41-47)* 16

Session 3   Faithfulness in Persecution *(Acts 5:21,25-35,38-42)* 26

Session 4   Obedience to the Spirit *(Acts 8:26-40)* 36

Session 5   Transformation Through the Gospel *(Acts 9:3-9,15-20)* 46

Session 6   Salvation Is for Everyone *(Acts 10:9-16,43-48)* 56

Leader Guide 66

Tips for Leading a Group 78

JESUS GIVES THE MISSION

Jesus assigned His followers the task of telling everyone about Him and His message.

ABOUT THE BOOK OF ACTS

As promised by Jesus, the Holy Spirit filled believers with His presence and power. For this reason many Bible students refer to this beloved Bible book as The Acts of the Holy Spirit. Through the power of the Spirit, the gospel message was proclaimed everywhere, and lives were transformed. That same reality continues for believers today.

AUTHOR

The writer of Acts didn't identify himself by name. However, clues within the book and its clear connection to the Gospel of Luke have led most evangelical Bible scholars to conclude that Luke, a physician and missionary associate of Paul (see Col. 4:14), wrote both the Third Gospel and Acts. He addressed both works to Theophilus (see Luke 1:3; Acts 1:1), and in Acts 1:1-2 he referred to the Gospel as his "first narrative ... about all that Jesus began to do and teach until the day He was taken up." Luke thus wrote Acts as a sequel to the Third Gospel. He tied the two works together by reporting at the end of the Gospel and again at the beginning of Acts the Lord's promise about the Holy Spirit (see Luke 24:49; Acts 1:1-8), as well as Jesus' ascension into heaven (see Luke 24:50-53; Acts 1:9-11).

DATE

Bible students hold differing views about the date Luke wrote Acts. One view (the view I hold) is that Acts was written in the early 60s. This view takes note that Luke made no mention in Acts of the Jerusalem temple's destruction in A.D. 70 or of the persecution of Christians instigated by Nero in A.D. 64. It seems probable that Luke would have mentioned these events if he had written after they occurred. Others, however, hold to a date of writing sometime around the temple's destruction in A.D. 70 or even as late as the mid-80s.

PURPOSE

Luke stated up front his purpose in writing Acts. He wanted to present an accurate narrative of the events surrounding Jesus' life on earth and the continuing influence of His ministry and message. Embedded within that purpose was an effort to defend the faith against assertions on the one hand that Christianity was a political movement against Rome and on the other hand that Christians were only a sect of Judaism.

"WE TALK OF THE SECOND COMING; HALF THE WORLD HAS NEVER HEARD OF THE FIRST."
—Oswald J. Smith

➤ ACTS 1:1-11

Think About It

Observe the promises Jesus made to the apostles in this passage. How are the promises connected to one another?

Identify the actions the apostles were to take. How are these actions related to the promises?

1 I wrote the first narrative, Theophilus, about all that Jesus began to do and teach **2** until the day He was taken up, after He had given orders through the Holy Spirit to the apostles He had chosen. **3** After He had suffered, He also presented Himself alive to them by many convincing proofs, appearing to them during 40 days and speaking about the kingdom of God. **4** While He was together with them, He commanded them not to leave Jerusalem, but to wait for the Father's promise. "This," He said, "is what you heard from Me; **5** for John baptized with water, but you will be baptized with the Holy Spirit not many days from now." **6** So when they had come together, they asked Him, "Lord, are You restoring the kingdom to Israel at this time?" **7** He said to them, "It is not for you to know times or periods that the Father has set by His own authority. **8** But you will receive power when the Holy Spirit has come on you, and you will be My witnesses in Jerusalem, in all Judea and Samaria, and to the ends of the earth." **9** After He had said this, He was taken up as they were watching, and a cloud took Him out of their sight. **10** While He was going, they were gazing into heaven, and suddenly two men in white clothes stood by them. **11** They said, "Men of Galilee, why do you stand looking up into heaven? This Jesus, who has been taken from you into heaven, will come in the same way that you have seen Him going into heaven."

❯ UNDERSTAND THE CONTEXT

USE THE FOLLOWING PAGES TO PREPARE FOR YOUR GROUP TIME.

The opening chapter of Acts pulses with expectation. It promises a dynamic sequel to the gospel story "about all that Jesus began to do and teach" (1:1). Luke assured his readers that the resurrected Lord Jesus, having ascended to the Father, was nevertheless continuing His redemptive mission on earth. He would do so through the Holy Spirit's living in, guiding, and empowering His followers "in Jerusalem, in all Judea and Samaria, and to the ends of the earth" (v. 8).

Luke reported the risen Lord's final instructions to His apostles: to remain in Jerusalem until they received the Holy Spirit (see vv. 4-5). Their mission would require supernatural enablement; it could not be accomplished on the basis of human energy and effort. The apostles wondered if Jesus' instruction signaled the imminent restoration of Israel as a political kingdom, but Jesus clarified the mission: they were to be His witnesses throughout the world (see vv. 6-8). Jesus then ascended into heaven, and two angels assured the watching apostles that He would one day return in the same way He had left them (see vv. 9-11).

In the remainder of Acts 1, Luke reported the process by which the community of disciples, now numbering about 120 people, restored the number of apostles to 12 after Judas the betrayer's death. The group flourished in an atmosphere of unity, so Peter led them to recommend worthy potential replacements, to pray about the decision, and then to select the new member of the twelve by casting lots. Trusting God's guidance, the group selected Matthias to join the apostles (see vv. 12-26).

› EXPLORE THE TEXT

THE REMEMBERED PROMISE (Acts 1:1-5)

¹I wrote the first narrative, Theophilus, about all that Jesus began to do and teach ²until the day He was taken up, after He had given orders through the Holy Spirit to the apostles He had chosen. ³After He had suffered, He also presented Himself alive to them by many convincing proofs, appearing to them during 40 days and speaking about the kingdom of God. ⁴While He was together with them, He commanded them not to leave Jerusalem, but to wait for the Father's promise. "This," He said, "is what you heard from Me; ⁵for John baptized with water, but you will be baptized with the Holy Spirit not many days from now."

Luke reminded Theophilus (see p. 7) that the first narrative he wrote (the Gospel of Luke) had focused on the life, actions, and teachings of Jesus during His time on earth. Some Bible students understand the phrase "most honorable Theophilus" in Luke 1:3 to suggest that this individual was an important Roman official (compare the descriptive phrases used in Acts 23:26; 26:25).

Luke reported that Jesus had given orders through the Holy Spirit to the apostles. The term *apostles* literally refers to those who have been appointed and sent out on a mission. The Commander giving the orders was Jesus. The Holy Spirit was the presence of God who would guide the apostles and empower them to carry out the mission.

Luke emphasized two key truths to reinforce his readers' faith in Jesus. First, after Jesus suffered and died on the cross, He also presented Himself alive. Jesus' resurrection was real and true, authenticated by many convincing proofs. The Greek word translated *proofs* refers to a certainty that can be confirmed by evidence. The resurrection of Jesus was confirmed when He appeared to multiple individuals and groups in the 40 days after His tomb was found to be empty (see 1 Cor. 15:4-8).

The second truth Luke emphasized was the centrality of the kingdom of God. God gave birth to the church for the purpose of expanding His kingdom. Faithful Jews longed for God to restore Israel to its former national glory. Jesus taught, however, that He inaugurated God's righteous reign through His ministry and mission.

Jesus commanded the apostles not to leave Jerusalem until further notice. What was so significant about their staying in Jerusalem? This city was the epicenter of Jewish worship and temple sacrifices. Centuries earlier the prophet Joel had predicted the outpouring of the Holy Spirit in Jerusalem and a subsequent spiritual awakening (see Joel 2:28-32). Furthermore, Jerusalem was the location of the death and resurrection of Jesus. For these reasons He instructed His apostles to remain in the city until they could boldly announce the fulfillment of the Father's promise.

What makes it difficult to wait for the Lord to prepare us to fulfill His purposes? What are the rewards of waiting?

THE RESURRECTION PROCLAIMED (Acts 1:6-8)

⁶So when they had come together, they asked Him, "Lord, are You restoring the kingdom to Israel at this time?" ⁷He said to them, "It is not for you to know times or periods that the Father has set by His own authority. ⁸But you will receive power when the Holy Spirit has come on you, and you will be My witnesses in Jerusalem, in all Judea and Samaria, and to the ends of the earth."

BIBLE SKILL
*Compare passages
with related concepts.*

Read Matthew 28:18-20;
Mark 16:15-16; Luke
24:46-49; and John 20:21.
Compare those passages
to what Luke recorded in
Acts 1:6-8. Take note of
similar themes, teachings,
and directives. How do
the passages complement
one another?

When the risen Lord spoke to His apostles about the kingdom of God, they were understandably curious (and perhaps confused) about what this meant. Jesus would have to clarify for the apostles that the kingdom of God centered in Him, not in a national entity. The kingdom of God is the reign of His grace and power in the lives of those who believe in Jesus. He declared that it was both futile and distracting from the real mission for the apostles to dwell on times or periods that were beyond their control. The Lord commissioned us to live faithfully each day, passionately proclaiming the gospel and making disciples, not to speculate about God's end-time calendar.

The mission of testifying to the resurrection was a task so enormous that the apostles needed supernatural ability. The power Jesus promised to His apostles was inseparable from their assigned mission. Witnesses are individuals who are compelled to tell others something they know to be true. Because the apostles knew Jesus had conquered sin and death through His death and resurrection, they were compelled to tell this good news. The content of the apostles' testimony focused on Jesus' death and resurrection. The cross pointed to Jesus' victory over sin. The resurrection pointed to His victory over death and the grave, as well as His validation as God's Son. Like the apostles and the early church, believers today are commissioned to bear witness to a world-changing historical event.

What hinders believers from fulfilling their assignment to testify about Jesus' presence in their lives? What role does the Holy Spirit play in helping believers share the gospel?

THE RETURN PORTRAYED (Acts 1:9-11)

⁹**After He had said this, He was taken up as they were watching, and a cloud took Him out of their sight. ¹⁰While He was going, they were gazing into heaven, and suddenly two men in white clothes stood by them. ¹¹They said, "Men of Galilee, why do you stand looking up into heaven? This Jesus, who has been taken from you into heaven, will come in the same way that you have seen Him going into heaven."**

Jesus' ascension demonstrated the Father's pleasure in welcoming the Son back into the glory of heaven (see John 17:4-5). It bridged the gap between the atoning work of Christ on the cross and His heavenly ministry as High Priest (see Heb. 8:1). Furthermore, the ascension opened the way for Jesus' power and presence to continue in His followers through the Holy Spirit. It was for their benefit that He would return to heaven and the Spirit would come to them (see John 16:7). Finally, the ascension underscored the fact that Jesus had given His apostles (and the church) a mission as His ambassadors.

As Jesus ascended into heaven, the apostles were gazing into heaven so intently that they didn't notice the appearance of two men in white clothes. The context strongly suggests these two men were angels whom God sent to assure the apostles about Jesus' future return. The two angels' question included a gentle rebuke. Instead of remaining in that place and looking up into heaven, the apostles needed to obey Jesus' command to stay in Jerusalem and prepare to get involved in the business of His mission. As motivation, the apostles were to keep in mind that one day their Master would come in the same way they had seen Him ascend into heaven. That is, He will return personally, bodily, visibly, and victoriously.

How can believers get caught gazing when they need to be obeying the Lord? What role does witnessing play in preparing for Jesus' return?

❯ OBEY THE TEXT

Believers follow Christ and point others to Him through the power of the Holy Spirit. In obedience and love, believers are to share the gospel with others. Believers are to live in light of Jesus' lordship and in anticipation of His return.

What is your group doing to point others to Jesus? What role do you play in helping the group point others to Jesus? Discuss ways your group can be more intentional in spreading the gospel to the ends of the earth.

What factors cause you to hesitate in fulfilling the mission of being Jesus' witness? What steps can you take to overcome your hesitation and obey the Lord's command to be a witness?

Record the names or initials of people with whom you could share the gospel. Ask God to help you find a way to talk with each person listed. Begin to act on what He reveals to you.

MEMORIZE

"You will receive power when the Holy Spirit has come on you, and you will be My witnesses in Jerusalem, in all Judea and Samaria, and to the ends of the earth." Acts 1:8

USE THE SPACE PROVIDED TO MAKE OBSERVATIONS AND RECORD PRAYER
REQUESTS DURING THE GROUP EXPERIENCE FOR THIS SESSION.

MY THOUGHTS

Record insights and questions from the group experience.

MY RESPONSE

Note specific ways you'll put into practice the truth explored this week.

MY PRAYERS

List specific prayer needs and answers to remember this week.

THE CHURCH IS BORN

The impact of the gospel is seen in the power and unity found among Jesus' followers.

❯ UNDERSTAND THE CONTEXT

USE THE FOLLOWING PAGES TO PREPARE FOR YOUR GROUP TIME.

Pentecost, also known as the Feast of Weeks, was one of the three major Jewish festivals observed annually. Occurring 50 days after the Passover feast, Pentecost was a joyous celebration marking the completion of the grain harvest. It thus attracted Jews and proselytes from all over the Roman Empire to make a pilgrimage to Jerusalem for the festivities. No one could have imagined, though, the supernatural power that would be unleashed during the first Pentecost following Jesus' crucifixion and resurrection.

The arrival of the Holy Spirit marked the formal beginning of the church. The Spirit ignited people's lives with such power that they were able to declare the message of the gospel and be understood in at least 15 different languages (see Acts 2:1-13).

Acts 2:14-40 records the sermon Peter delivered to the crowd in Jerusalem. Peter explained that what had happened was nothing less than the divine fulfillment of Old Testament prophecies about the dawning of the new messianic age. He quoted from the Book of Joel and from two messianic psalms (Pss. 16; 110), then concluded with a passionate declaration that Jesus—the very One whom the Jews had recently crucified—was both Lord and Messiah.

Peter was filled with the Spirit, but he was also filled with God's Word. As a result, those who heard his message were compelled to reach a verdict about Jesus in their hearts. Consequently, Peter urged his listeners to repent of their sins and be baptized as a testimony of their surrender to Christ.

> "GOD'S WORK DONE IN GOD'S WAY WILL NEVER LACK GOD'S SUPPLY."
> —Hudson Taylor

The response to Peter's message was staggering, as three thousand people became believers. This burgeoning community of Christ followers became actively engaged in listening to the apostles teach, in talking to and encouraging one another, in taking meals together, and in praying together. They demonstrated Christlike love for one another, and they acted with grace toward others in Jerusalem. Furthermore, their example continues to shine across the centuries and to beckon churches today to take up the mission of Jesus.

❯ ACTS 2:1-4,41-47

Think About It

Identify words or phrases that describe things done by the early church. In what ways do you see these actions being done in your church?

What words or phrases point to the attitudes of the members of the early church? How are these attitudes connected to the actions you identified?

1 When the day of Pentecost had arrived, they were all together in one place. **2** Suddenly a sound like that of a violent rushing wind came from heaven, and it filled the whole house where they were staying. **3** And tongues, like flames of fire that were divided, appeared to them and rested on each one of them. **4** Then they were all filled with the Holy Spirit and began to speak in different languages, as the Spirit gave them ability for speech.

41 So those who accepted his message were baptized, and that day about 3,000 people were added to them. **42** And they devoted themselves to the apostles' teaching, to the fellowship, to the breaking of bread, and to the prayers. **43** Then fear came over everyone, and many wonders and signs were being performed through the apostles. **44** Now all the believers were together and held all things in common. **45** They sold their possessions and property and distributed the proceeds to all, as anyone had a need. **46** Every day they devoted themselves to meeting together in the temple complex, and broke bread from house to house. They ate their food with a joyful and humble attitude, **47** praising God and having favor with all the people. And every day the Lord added to them those who were being saved.

❯ EXPLORE THE TEXT

THE SPIRIT GIVEN (Acts 2:1-4)

¹When the day of Pentecost had arrived, they were all together in one place. ²Suddenly a sound like that of a violent rushing wind came from heaven, and it filled the whole house where they were staying. ³And tongues, like flames of fire that were divided, appeared to them and rested on each one of them. ⁴Then they were all filled with the Holy Spirit and began to speak in different languages, as the Spirit gave them ability for speech.

The word Pentecost comes from a Greek term meaning *fifty*. Originally, Pentecost was known as the Feast of Weeks because it occurred seven weeks and one day after Passover (see Lev. 23:15-16). This was one of three annual pilgrimage feasts when all Jewish males were expected to travel to Jerusalem and present an offering of firstfruits to the Lord (see Deut. 16:16). The unity of the believers testified to their cohesive focus on Jesus. He consumed their attention. He dominated their thoughts. When we as believers rivet our passion on Jesus in unified obedience, the impact of our witness can be phenomenal.

Why is unity of purpose and focus critical for the church? What's the connection between a focus on Jesus and unity in the church?

The prayer meeting (see Acts 1:14) of believers was suddenly interrupted by a sound similar to the roar of a powerful wind. In the Old Testament wind often represented God's invading presence (see Ps. 104:3; Ezek. 37:9-10). Furthermore, wind signified God's power to tear down and build up. In addition to the sudden and powerful sound, tongues like flames of fire settled on the believers in a visual representation of the Holy Spirit. Tongues represented human speech and the communication of the gospel. Fire indicated the purifying presence of God. The fire associated with God's presence in the Old Testament was reserved for unique occasions, but the image of fire that rested with believers on the Day of Pentecost pointed to the abiding presence of the Holy Spirit. John the Baptist testified that Christ would immerse believers with the Holy Spirit and fire (see Luke 3:16). Pentecost served as the public fulfillment of that prophecy.

Two important truths can be seen here. First, the power of the Holy Spirit enabled believers to act bravely and to speak boldly. Second, as the context of this passage confirms, their words were clear and understandable in the multiple languages and dialects of the hearers.

What forms of evidence show that the Holy Spirit indwells a believer?

DEVOTED (Acts 2:41-42)

⁴¹So those who accepted his message were baptized, and that day about 3,000 people were added to them. ⁴²And they devoted themselves to the apostles' teaching, to the fellowship, to the breaking of bread, and to the prayers.

The picture Luke presented about the beginning of the church is beautifully compelling. The Greek word translated *accepted* (see. v. 41) carries the idea of a glad reception. The new believers delightfully embraced the truth about Jesus and then demonstrated their obedience publicly through the act of baptism. The inward change and the outward rite underscore the proper order and sequence: faith (conversion) first, then obedience (baptism). In other words, these new believers were not saved by being baptized. Rather, they were saved when they repented and believed in Jesus. Their baptism was an act of obedience as believers and a testimony of what had occurred in their hearts.

The first activity of the believers' devotion involved spiritual growth through the apostles' teaching. The believers submitted themselves to godly instruction from the apostles. This instruction was life-transforming truth that Jesus had taught the apostles. The second activity the believers were devoted to was fellowship. As a family of faith, the first believers celebrated their shared salvation through Jesus. They practiced a dynamic connection to one another because they were joined by a common faith in the Savior. Third, the believers practiced the breaking of bread together. This could refer either to eating meals together in fellow believers' homes or to partaking of the Lord's Supper in worship. In either case the practice enhanced the believers' shared life in Christ. Fourth, the early believers devoted themselves to prayer. Jews were accustomed to regular times of prayer each day. Jewish believers continued this discipline as Christ's followers, but prayer took on a deeper significance because they could now pray about anything in the name of Jesus (see John 14:13-14).

How does participation in these activities promote unity in a church? Can a church be unified without focusing on these elements? Explain.

> **KEY DOCTRINE**
> *The Church*
>
> A New Testament church of the Lord Jesus Christ is an autonomous local congregation of baptized believers, associated by covenant in the faith and fellowship of the gospel; observing the two ordinances of Christ; governed by His laws; exercising the gifts, rights, and privileges invested in them by His Word; and seeking to extend the gospel to the ends of the earth

TOGETHER (Acts 2:43-47a)

⁴³Then fear came over everyone, and many wonders and signs were being performed through the apostles. ⁴⁴Now all the believers were together and held all things in common. ⁴⁵They sold their possessions and property and distributed the proceeds to all, as anyone had a need. ⁴⁶Every day they devoted themselves to meeting together in the temple complex, and broke bread from house to house. They ate their food with a joyful and humble attitude, ⁴⁷praising God and having favor with all the people.

The purpose of miraculous activity was to draw attention to the gospel message and to validate the gospel messengers. The Bible instructs us in many places to fear God because doing so humbles our ego and

BIBLE SKILL

Look at the original language of a text.

Do a concept study of the Greek term *koinonia*, rendered *fellowship* in Acts 2:42, by considering other appearances of the term in the New Testament. (English words may differ in translations.)

Find and read the following verses: 1 Corinthians 1:9; 10:16 (participation); 2 Corinthians 6:14 (in common); 9:13 (sharing); Galatians 2:9; Philippians 1:5 (partnership); 2:1; 3:10; Hebrews 13:16 (to share); 1 John 1:3, 6-7. How does each verse help you better understand the nature of the relationship of koinonia among believers?

magnifies His attributes. Fear of the Lord is a disposition of the heart in response to His awesome power.

Scripture exhorts us to worship together, to encourage one another, and to love and honor others. These biblical activities are fulfilled in a shared passion for Christ and in a mutual bond with one another. The believers living in Jerusalem demonstrated a deep commitment to Jesus that overflowed in mutual support for one another. As needs arose, they sold their possessions and property to help other believers. There was no expectation that new believers must immediately relinquish all their possessions on conversion. The emphasis in the early church was on compassionate ministry, not asceticism or political socialism. When Christians discovered that someone was facing great need, the grace of Christ moved them to sell items to help relieve the hardship.

At this early stage Christ's followers continued to worship within the structure of their Jewish heritage. They had opportunities in that setting to interact with other Jews and to testify about Jesus. The Greek term rendered *together* (see v. 44) refers to more than the proximity of people to one another; it speaks of people being united in spirit and purpose. Believers were united in their faith in Jesus and in their mission of telling others about the gospel.

The early Christians' life together also included visits into one another's homes for shared meals. Such occasions were marked by "a joyful and humble attitude" (v. 46) on the part of believers. Their lives weren't easy and trouble free, yet the Spirit filled them with joy and hope. As believers today, we sometimes think solemn reverence is more important to the Lord than overt gladness. Certainly there are a time and a place for both, but Scripture teaches us that joy is as much an expression of sincere worship as is subdued seriousness. When we reflect on the forgiveness of our sins through Christ and the eternal hope we have because of His resurrection from the dead, there are more than enough reasons to be filled with gladness and generosity.

Gratitude and goodwill overflowed in abundance. The believers praised God with energetic gratitude and won the respect of others by their joyful, humble fellowship. A vibrant church shines in two directions: (1) upward in adoration to God for the gift of His Son and (2) outward in grace toward others. Both directions are vital.

What does a consistent display of sincere adoration of God and grace toward others show about what a church believes about God?

GROWING (Acts 2:47b)

⁴⁷And every day the Lord added to them those who were being saved.

The early church in Jerusalem was a healthy, witnessing community. Believers testified about Jesus. They related to and connected with other citizens in the city. The Holy Spirit used their testimony to draw unbelievers to faith, and the Lord added to the church "those who were being saved." In other words, the early church experienced both qualitative and quantitative growth. Believers grew in their faith, and more people placed their faith in Jesus as the Messiah. The people being added to the church were those whom the Lord had saved by grace through faith in Jesus. The new believers weren't being saved by joining the church. The church is the community of those who have been saved by faith in Jesus Christ (see Acts 4:10-12).

What does Acts 2:1-4,41-47 teach about the relationship between church growth and church health? How do they enhance each other?

❯ OBEY THE TEXT

Every believer is to be a witness. Believers are enabled by the Holy Spirit to fulfill their God-given mission. To be spiritually healthy, believers need to be connected to other believers. In churches believers can live life together, meet one another's needs, and worship together. God's demonstration of Himself through believers can cause unbelievers to become curious about God and His power. When placed in situations where unbelievers are asking questions, believers can seize opportunities to share Jesus.

If a dozen people were randomly selected to observe you every day for one week, how might they evaluate your devotion to Jesus? Based on this session's Bible passage, what do you think needs to improve in your devotion to Jesus?

What are you doing to help strengthen unity in your church and Bible-study group? Identify some strategies you can apply to deepen and enhance your relationships with others in your congregation and group.

Reflect on ways living life with other believers helps you share the gospel. What can you do to help motivate other believers to share the gospel?

MEMORIZE

"Every day they devoted themselves to meeting together in the temple complex, and broke bread from house to house. They ate their food with a joyful and humble attitude." Acts 2:46

USE THE SPACE PROVIDED TO MAKE OBSERVATIONS AND RECORD PRAYER
REQUESTS DURING THE GROUP EXPERIENCE FOR THIS SESSION.

MY THOUGHTS

Record insights and questions from the group experience.

MY RESPONSE

Note specific ways you'll put into practice the truth explored this week.

MY PRAYERS

List specific prayer needs and answers to remember this week.

FAITHFULNESS IN PERSECUTION

The Holy Spirit gives believers courage to proclaim the truth.

UNDERSTAND THE CONTEXT

USE THE FOLLOWING PAGES TO PREPARE FOR YOUR GROUP TIME.

Peter and John demonstrated spiritual courage by healing a crippled man in Jesus' name at one of the temple gates (see Acts 3:1-10). The healing stirred a lot of astonishment among the people. Peter seized the opportunity to explain that the source of the power for the miracle was the risen Christ. Moreover, Peter challenged the crowd to repent of their sins and place their faith in Jesus (see vv. 11-26).

The boldness of Peter and John in publicly proclaiming the gospel put them in direct conflict with the temple authorities. The two were arrested and brought before the Sanhedrin for questioning (see 4:1-12). The council warned Peter and John not to continue preaching in Jesus' name, but Peter courageously answered that their testimony about Jesus was a matter of being obedient to God. "When they observed the boldness of Peter and John and realized that they were uneducated and untrained men, they were amazed and recognized that they had been with Jesus" (v. 13). Unable to find a way to punish the two apostles, the council released them with additional threats (see vv. 14-22).

> "I WANT TO INVEST MY LIFE IN SOMETHING THAT IS GOING TO OUTLIVE ME."—*Vance H. Pitman*

Temple leaders decided that new measures had to be taken against the followers of Christ. Thus, they had the apostles jailed to await a hearing before the Sanhedrin. When the Sanhedrin convened and ordered the apostles to be brought in, it was reported with surprise that the apostles not only were absent from their cells but were standing in the temple courtyards teaching the people.

The police then retrieved the apostles and escorted them before the council, whereupon the high priest reminded them of the council's demand that they stop their evangelistic activities. Speaking for the apostles once again, Peter boldly explained that they were witnesses of what God had done in Christ. They had no option; they were compelled to obey God and to tell the people the truth about Jesus and the gospel (see 5:17-32). Irate council members wanted to kill the apostles, but a Pharisee named Gamaliel persuaded them otherwise. He advised the council to take a cautious approach. As a result, the apostles were flogged, threatened, and released (see vv. 33-42).

▶ ACTS 5:21,25-35,38-42

21 When the high priest and those who were with him arrived, they convened the Sanhedrin—the full Senate of the sons of Israel—and sent orders to the jail to have them brought.

25 Someone came and reported to them, "Look! The men you put in jail are standing in the temple complex and teaching the people." **26** Then the commander went with the temple police and brought them in without force, because they were afraid the people might stone them. **27** After they brought them in, they had them stand before the Sanhedrin, and the high priest asked, **28** "Didn't we strictly order you not to teach in this name? And look, you have filled Jerusalem with your teaching and are determined to bring this man's blood on us!" **29** But Peter and the apostles replied, "We must obey God rather than men. **30** The God of our fathers raised up Jesus, whom you had murdered by hanging Him on a tree. **31** God exalted this man to His right hand as ruler and Savior, to grant repentance to Israel, and forgiveness of sins. **32** We are witnesses of these things, and so is the Holy Spirit whom God has given to those who obey Him." **33** When they heard this, they were enraged and wanted to kill them. **34** A Pharisee named Gamaliel, a teacher of the law who was respected by all the people, stood up in the Sanhedrin and ordered the men to be taken outside for a little while. **35** He said to them, "Men of Israel, be careful about what you're going to do to these men.

38 "And now, I tell you, stay away from these men and leave them alone. For if this plan or this work is of men, it will be overthrown; **39** but if it is of God, you will not be able to overthrow them. You may even be found fighting against God." So they were persuaded by him. **40** After they called in the apostles and had them flogged, they ordered them not to speak in the name of Jesus and released them. **41** Then they went out from the presence of the Sanhedrin, rejoicing that they were counted worthy to be dishonored on behalf of the Name. **42** Every day in the temple complex, and in various homes, they continued teaching and proclaiming the good news that Jesus is the Messiah.

Think About It

Take note of words or phrases that reveal the attitudes and motives of the religious leaders.

Then identify words or phrases that reveal the attitudes and motives of the apostles.

How do the lists compare and contrast?

EXPLORE THE TEXT

RETURNING TO THE SCENE (Acts 5:25-28)

²⁵Someone came and reported to them, "Look! The men you put in jail are standing in the temple complex and teaching the people." ²⁶Then the commander went with the temple police and brought them in without force, because they were afraid the people might stone them. ²⁷After they brought them in, they had them stand before the Sanhedrin, and the high priest asked, ²⁸"Didn't we strictly order you not to teach in this name? And look, you have filled Jerusalem with your teaching and are determined to bring this man's blood on us!"

After having been thrown in jail to await the council's convening and then miraculously being delivered by an angel, the apostles were once again teaching in the temple courtyards (see vv. 17-21a). The council convened for the hearing, but the apostles were not in the jail (see vv. 21b-24). An unidentified person came and reported to the Sanhedrin that the apostles were at that moment standing in the temple complex and teaching the people. The temple police once again detained the apostles but this time without force. The people were sympathetic to the apostles. A strong-arm tactic might enrage the crowd.

Behind closed doors the high priest exhibited his animosity toward the apostles. He reminded the apostles of the council's prohibition against teaching about Jesus. Notably, the high priest didn't ask how the apostles had escaped from the jail.

The council had a deep-seated fear that their place and control over the people were slipping away. They took great offense at the apostles' insistence that the religious leaders had Jesus' blood on their hands. However, the apostles weren't speaking or acting with vengeance. They were testifying to the truth. The Jewish leaders had the same opportunity as others to hear, repent, and trust God's redeeming plan through Jesus the Messiah.

What motivated the religious leaders to silence the apostles? How is that motive seen in today's world?

STANDING THEIR GROUND *(Acts 5:29-32)*

29But Peter and the apostles replied, "We must obey God rather than men. 30The God of our fathers raised up Jesus, whom you had murdered by hanging Him on a tree. 31God exalted this man to His right hand as ruler and Savior, to grant repentance to Israel, and forgiveness of sins. 32We are witnesses of these things, and so is the Holy Spirit whom God has given to those who obey Him."

Again Peter served as the speaker for the apostles. He explained that as witnesses of the truth, the apostles had no choice but to obey God rather than men. His point was that for followers of Christ, God's commands take precedence over everything else.

God had raised up Jesus, whom the Jewish leaders had rejected and crucified. The expression "hanging Him on a tree" (v. 30) was Peter's way of saying the Jewish leaders considered Jesus' crucifixion to be a sign of God's curse on Jesus (see Deut. 21:22-23). By resurrecting Jesus, God in fact vindicated His Son and the gospel.

Peter stated that God exalted Jesus to His right hand as Ruler and Savior because He had defeated sin and death, opening the way for our salvation. That salvation is received through repentance and the forgiveness of sins.

Peter again stressed that the apostles had been witnesses of Jesus' sinless life, atoning death, and victorious resurrection. Furthermore, the Holy Spirit was a divine witness to these events, and the Spirit now indwelled and empowered the followers of Christ in their mission to preach and teach the gospel. Therefore, the apostles could not and would not obey the Sanhedrin.

How would you summarize Peter's defense? Do you think Peter's speech was more convincing or more convicting? Explain.

WAITING DURING DELIBERATIONS
(Acts 5:33-35,38-39)

³³**When they heard this, they were enraged and wanted to kill them. ³⁴A Pharisee named Gamaliel, a teacher of the law who was respected by all the people, stood up in the Sanhedrin and ordered the men to be taken outside for a little while. ³⁵He said to them, "Men of Israel, be careful about what you're going to do to these men."**

Like a blade, Peter's preaching could be soul-piercingly sharp (see Acts 2:37; 4:1-2). It could evoke either repentance or rage, depending on the hearer's attitude. Most of the council members had the latter reaction to Peter's testimony. They had used their influence with the Roman authorities to get rid of Jesus (so they thought); they could do the same with Jesus' followers.

One of the more influential and popular council members, a Pharisee named Gamaliel, offered a different approach. He was concerned about the council's handing down more death sentences against the apostles. The apostles enjoyed great favor with the people at the moment. To propose his alternative response, Gamaliel directed that the apostles be taken outside the meeting area.

Gamaliel urged the irate council members to exercise caution. Issuing death sentences could stir up a popular uprising against the council. Furthermore, the council might find itself in opposition to God.

BIBLE SKILL

Memorize a verse and consider its practical implications.

Memorize Acts 4:12 in your preferred translation. Paraphrase the verse in your own words. Record three reasons Jesus is the only way of salvation. Record two commonly held cultural beliefs the verse challenges. How does the belief that Christ alone can save affect your view of missions?

³⁸"And now, I tell you, stay away from these men and leave them alone. For if this plan or this work is of men, it will be overthrown; ³⁹but if it is of God, you will not be able to overthrow them. You may even be found fighting against God." So they were persuaded by him.

Gamaliel knew of two recent, failed revolutionary movements (see vv. 36-37). He proposed to the council that Jesus' followers would have a similar outcome if their movement was merely of human origin.

Gamaliel also advised the council to consider the position they would be in if what was occurring had its origins in the will of God. Gamaliel's arguments thus convinced the council to spare the apostles.

What wisdom do you see in Gamaliel's proposal to the council? How might his words help believers today?

REJOICING FOR THE OPPORTUNITY (Acts 5:40-42)

⁴⁰After they called in the apostles and had them flogged, they ordered them not to speak in the name of Jesus and released them. ⁴¹Then they went out from the presence of the Sanhedrin, rejoicing that they were counted worthy to be dishonored on behalf of the Name. ⁴²Every day in the temple complex, and in various homes, they continued teaching and proclaiming the good news that Jesus is the Messiah.

The Old Testament law allowed for various forms of punishment, including the practice of administering public beatings (see Deut. 25:1-3). Having been persuaded by Gamaliel to back off their demand for death, the council imposed two forms of punishment. First, they had the apostles flogged. Such a whipping was meant to humiliate, injure, and scar the victim. Second, they were ordered not to speak in the name of Jesus.

The council's punishment didn't have the desired effect. The apostles walked away from their beatings not cowering and crying but, rather, rejoicing that they were counted worthy to suffer shame and a beating in Jesus' name. They viewed their mistreatment as confirmation of their devotion. They bore no shame for being faithful to Jesus.

Neither did the apostles obey the order to stop teaching about Jesus. If anything, they increased their gospel activity. They taught daily. They taught both in the temple area and in people's homes. They didn't stop declaring the good news that Jesus is the Messiah. They faithfully and courageously obeyed the Lord's express command to go and tell everyone to repent and believe.

How can opposition to the gospel produce courage in believers?
How does opposition provide a platform for the gospel to be shared?

❯ OBEY THE TEXT

Believers are to faithfully stand for Jesus when facing personal challenges. The truth of the gospel is trustworthy and can be shared with confidence. Believers can rejoice when persecuted, realizing that the gospel is proclaimed in the process.

Consider times in your life when someone challenged your faith. How did you respond? What can you learn from the apostles' example to help you respond when facing opposition in the future?

Reflect on ways you've found the gospel to be trustworthy. How do these ways give you confidence to share the gospel? Identify one person with whom you can share about the trustworthiness of the gospel this week.

Share with others in your Bible-study group about situations in which you've faced opposition to your belief in Jesus. Record insights gained from one another's stories. Take time to thank God for the opportunity to present the gospel while standing up to opposition.

MEMORIZE

"Peter and the apostles replied, 'We must obey God rather than men.' " Acts 5:29

USE THE SPACE PROVIDED TO MAKE OBSERVATIONS AND RECORD PRAYER
REQUESTS DURING THE GROUP EXPERIENCE FOR THIS SESSION.

MY THOUGHTS

Record insights and questions from the group experience.

MY RESPONSE

Note specific ways you'll put into practice the truth explored this week.

MY PRAYERS

List specific prayer needs and answers to remember this week.

OBEDIENCE TO THE SPIRIT

Opportunities to share the gospel message come through obedience.

UNDERSTAND THE CONTEXT

USE THE FOLLOWING PAGES TO PREPARE FOR YOUR GROUP TIME.

The martyrdom of Stephen set off a scorching outbreak of persecution against Christians in Jerusalem; it was led by Saul of Tarsus, a firebrand Pharisee (see Acts 8:1-3). Many believers were forced to flee the city and seek refuge in other places. Wherever they scattered, however, they took the gospel message with them (see v. 4).

Philip, who like Stephen had been among the seven men set apart to carry out the church's ministry to widows (see 6:5), went to the region of Samaria. There he began proclaiming Jesus as the Messiah. Philip's preaching was accompanied by powerful signs, including the expulsion of evil spirits from some people and the physical healing of others. A sense of joy spread over the whole area (see 8:5-8).

Among the Samaritan converts was a well-known former sorcerer named Simon. He professed to believe in Jesus and was baptized, yet he was astonished most by the miraculous works Philip performed (see vv. 9-13). When Peter and John came from Jerusalem to Samaria and laid hands on the new converts to receive the Holy Spirit, Simon offered to buy that power from the two apostles. Peter rebuked Simon and urged him to repent of making such a sinful request (see vv. 14-25).

Philip followed the Lord's direction to leave Samaria and go to a road running between Jerusalem and Gaza. There he came upon an Ethiopian, an important official in the royal court, who was reading a scroll of Isaiah as he rode along in his chariot. Philip greeted the man and soon had an opportunity to explain how Jesus fulfilled the prophecy that the man was reading. The Ethiopian declared his faith in Jesus, and Philip baptized him. The man then went on his way as a new believer, while Philip moved to other coastal towns, preaching the gospel everywhere he went (see vv. 26-40).

"SYMPATHY IS NO SUBSTITUTE FOR ACTION."

—David Livingstone

❯ ACTS 8:26-31,35,38-39

26 An angel of the Lord spoke to Philip: "Get up and go south to the road that goes down from Jerusalem to Gaza." (This is the desert road.) **27** So he got up and went. There was an Ethiopian man, a eunuch and high official of Candace, queen of the Ethiopians, who was in charge of her entire treasury. He had come to worship in Jerusalem **28** and was sitting in his chariot on his way home, reading the prophet Isaiah aloud. **29** The Spirit told Philip, "Go and join that chariot." **30** When Philip ran up to it, he heard him reading the prophet Isaiah, and said, "Do you understand what you're reading?" **31** "How can I," he said, "unless someone guides me?" So he invited Philip to come up and sit with him.

35 So Philip proceeded to tell him the good news about Jesus, beginning from that Scripture.

38 Then he ordered the chariot to stop, and both Philip and the eunuch went down into the water, and he baptized him. **39** When they came up out of the water, the Spirit of the Lord carried Philip away, and the eunuch did not see him any longer. But he went on his way rejoicing.

Think About It

Identify phrases in this passage that show the depth of Philip's daily walk with the Lord.

How did Philip's walk with the Lord influence his actions?

▶ EXPLORE THE TEXT

COMPELLED TO SEEK (Acts 8:26-29)

²⁶An angel of the Lord spoke to Philip: "Get up and go south to the road that goes down from Jerusalem to Gaza." (This is the desert road.) ²⁷So he got up and went. There was an Ethiopian man, a eunuch and high official of Candace, queen of the Ethiopians, who was in charge of her entire treasury. He had come to worship in Jerusalem ²⁸and was sitting in his chariot on his way home, reading the prophet Isaiah aloud. ²⁹The Spirit told Philip, "Go and join that chariot."

Like a storm wind that catches up seeds and then drops them far and wide onto new ground, the persecution against the church in Jerusalem scattered hosts of gospel witnesses into new areas. Wherever these believers went, they talked about the good news of Jesus Christ, which took root in many hearts. Luke gave an example of this phenomenon in the account of Philip in Samaria (see vv. 5-8). The gospel advanced in other ways too, including by what might be called divine appointments between an attentive, obedient believer and a spiritual seeker. Luke gave an example of this type of gospel advance in the account of Philip and the Ethiopian eunuch (see vv. 26-39).

Luke began the account by reporting that an angel of the Lord spoke to Philip. An angel is a messenger from God, so the instructions for Philip emphasize God's perfect timing and guidance, the urgency of evangelism, and God's expectation of obedience.

Moreover, the angel gave Philip clear details about the destination: he was to head south and go to a road that ran between Jerusalem and the city of Gaza near the Mediterranean coast. Yet the angel didn't reveal at this time the purpose of Philip's journey. So these details reveal not only the exactness of God's guidance but also the need for a believer to trust and obey the Lord step by step.

Notice the profound simplicity of Philip's response. He obeyed in faith, and he obeyed immediately. As believers today, we can learn a lot from Philip's obedience. God may prompt us to go to unexpected places or to prepare ourselves in unexpected ways to meet a strategic need. Traveling along the road in a horse-drawn chariot was an Ethiopian man. In biblical times the name Ethiopia was associated with the land of Cush in the upper Nile River valley rather than with the present-day nation of that name located at the southwestern end of the Red Sea.

Luke provided additional information about this Ethiopian man. First, he was a eunuch. In ancient Near Eastern societies this term often referred to a man in charge of a king's harem. The eunuch was rendered sexually impotent by means of castration. Over time the term also came to be used of men—usually royal officials—who served the queen or other female members of the royal court and who took a vow of sexual abstinence as part of their service.

Second, the man was a high official of Candace, the queen of the Ethiopians. Indeed, he was the queen's chief financial officer. As such, he played a key role in the financial well-being of the entire nation. Third, the man had been in Jerusalem to worship at the temple. This fact suggests the man was (or hoped to be) a proselyte to Judaism. The law of Moses forbade eunuchs from entering the Lord's assembly (see Deut. 23:1); however, the prophet Isaiah foresaw a day when eunuchs who obeyed God's Word would be welcomed into God's presence (see Isa. 56:3-5). Perhaps the Ethiopian found hope in reading these words of Isaiah.

The phrase "sitting in his chariot" (Acts 8:28) suggests that the chariot was large and had a driver. More significant, however, is the fact that the man was reading aloud from the prophet Isaiah as he rode along. This suggests the man was educated, was wealthy enough to own a handwritten copy of a biblical scroll, and was concerned enough about his spiritual condition that he traveled hundreds of miles to and from Jerusalem by chariot to find answers. A person truly thirsty for God will go to great lengths to satisfy that need. Once again Philip received a divine direction. Interestingly, this time the guidance came not through an angel but directly from the Spirit.

What are means the Lord uses today to direct believers in carrying out the gospel mission? How do faith and obedience factor into those means?

PREPARED TO SHARE (Acts 8:30-31,35)

³⁰**When Philip ran up to it, he heard him reading the prophet Isaiah, and said, "Do you understand what you're reading?"** ³¹**"How can I," he said, "unless someone guides me?" So he invited Philip to come up and sit with him.** ³⁵**So Philip proceeded to tell him the good news about Jesus, beginning from that Scripture.**

Philip followed the Holy Spirit's direction and ran to the chariot. Do you suppose that as he ran, Philip thought about potential obstacles that might hinder his witness?

Many believers today wrestle with similar kinds of thoughts and sometimes allow the fear of inadequacy to dampen their passion for witnessing. Philip's example encourages us as believers to trust and obey the Holy Spirit, for He is at work around those who need to hear the gospel, in the witnessing situations to which He has guided us, and in our own fearful hearts.

Philip initiated the encounter by watching and listening. He noticed the man was reading a passage aloud, and he listened closely enough to recognize the text was from Isaiah 53. Paying close attention to what captures another person's interest can often open a door of opportunity to talk about spiritual matters. Respect and flexibility are key qualities in effective evangelism. Also notice that Philip asked a respectful yet probing question. A good question can break down barriers and open the flow of communication about the gospel.

The doctrine of the clarity of Scripture teaches that the Bible can be understood by an ordinary reader. It isn't written in a secret code that only a select few can decipher. Yet neither is it a text of which each person's private interpretations are necessarily true and correct. Thus, the Ethiopian official invited Philip to come up and sit with him in the chariot. The official, an expert in financial matters, humbly welcomed an opportunity to learn from Philip what a key Bible passage meant.

Acts 8:32-33 reveals that the Ethiopian official was reading Isaiah 53:7-8, which speaks of the Messiah's unjust suffering and death. The sticking point for the Ethiopian seems to have hinged on the identification of the Suffering Messiah (see Acts 8:34).

Philip used this opening to tell the man the good news about Jesus. (Jesus' fulfillment of Old Testament prophecy is one of Luke's major themes in the Book of Acts.) A consistent Christian lifestyle and a respectful witnessing approach speak volumes about the Lord Jesus. Yet at some point a verbal presentation of the gospel is necessary so that unbelievers can hear and respond in faith to Jesus (see Rom. 10:14-17).

How did Philip use Scripture to point to Jesus? Why was it important for Philip to make this connection?

FOCUSED ON SALVATION (Acts 8:38-39)

38Then he ordered the chariot to stop, and both Philip and the eunuch went down into the water, and he baptized him. 39When they came up out of the water, the Spirit of the Lord carried Philip away, and the eunuch did not see him any longer. But he went on his way rejoicing.

It is possible that during his visit to Jerusalem, the official had seen converts baptized as followers of Christ. At some moment on his journey home, the Ethiopian believed in Jesus. He then wanted to know from Philip whether anything disqualified him, as it did in Judaism, from being baptized as a believer (see v. 36).

Because he professed faith in Jesus, nothing disqualified the Ethiopian eunuch from being baptized (see v. 37). Consequently, when they saw a body of water, the official commanded the chariot to stop, the two men went down into the water, and Philip baptized him. In the New Testament the significance of baptism is never isolated from the method—immersion in water. Baptism signifies a believer's identification with Christ in His death, burial, and resurrection. Baptism doesn't save anyone; Jesus alone saves.

How would you use this passage to explain baptism to someone? What other information would you need to give them a more complete picture?

After the Ethiopian's baptism the Holy Spirit carried Philip away to another place of service. Whether this was a miraculous exit or simply the way Luke described the two men's parting isn't clear. In any case the Ethiopian man went on his way rejoicing. Joy is a characteristic associated with faith in Jesus; it's a sign of new life.

❯ OBEY THE TEXT

Believers must recognize opportunities to share Jesus with others as directed by the Holy Spirit. Believers gain confidence to share their testimonies as they grow in their understanding of the Scriptures. Salvation is available to all who are willing to receive Jesus.

What barriers must you overcome to better recognize opportunities to share Jesus with others? Identify steps you will take to overcome a barrier.

Schedule time this week to search your Bible and to pray. Ask the Holy Spirit to reveal to you how you can network with others in your Bible-study group to share the gospel more effectively.

List questions you have that keep you from following Jesus. If you're already a follower of Jesus, list questions you had prior to making that commitment. How can you use those questions to strengthen your personal strategies for introducing someone to Jesus?

MEMORIZE

"Those who were scattered went on their way preaching the message of good news." Acts 8:4

MY THOUGHTS

Record insights and questions from the group experience.

_____
_____
_____
_____
_____
_____

MY RESPONSE

Note specific ways you'll put into practice the truth explored this week.

_____
_____
_____
_____
_____

MY PRAYERS

List specific prayer needs and answers to remember this week.

_____
_____
_____
_____
_____
_____

TRANSFORMATION THROUGH THE GOSPEL

God calls people to be His messengers, with the first step being a commitment to follow Christ.

UNDERSTAND THE CONTEXT

USE THE FOLLOWING PAGES TO PREPARE FOR YOUR GROUP TIME.

Saul intended to imprison the messengers of Jesus and thereby silence their message about Jesus. He secured documents of authority from the high priest in Jerusalem so that he could arrest believers living in Damascus and extradite them to Jerusalem (see Acts 9:1-2).

Saul's journey to Damascus was interrupted by a blinding light from heaven and the voice of Jesus asking Saul why he was persecuting Him. Jesus told him to get up and go into Damascus, where he would receive further instructions (see vv. 3-9).

At the same time, God commanded a believer named Ananias, who lived in Damascus, to go to the house where Saul was staying and pray for him. Understandably, Ananias was reluctant to do so because Saul's violent reputation was widely known. The Lord explained to Ananias that Saul was His chosen instrument to present the gospel message to Gentiles and Jews, as well as to kings (see vv. 10-16).

Ananias obeyed the Lord. He found Saul and prayed for him. Saul immediately regained his sight and was baptized. Soon after, Saul began testifying about Jesus in the synagogues and proclaiming Jesus as the Son of God and the Messiah (see vv. 17-22).

Some unbelieving Jews plotted to kill Saul and silence his witness, but his friends rescued him and escorted him out of Damascus at night. Saul returned to Jerusalem, where Barnabas befriended him and introduced him to the apostles. Another attempt by some Jews to kill Saul led the believers to escort him to Caesarea, where he was sent to Tarsus. Meanwhile, the church kept growing (see vv. 23-31).

"THE GOSPEL IS ONLY GOOD NEWS IF IT GETS THERE IN TIME."
—Carl F. H. Henry

➤ ACTS 9:3-9,15-20

Think About It

Identify and answer the questions Jesus asked in this passage.

3 As [Saul] traveled and was nearing Damascus, a light from heaven suddenly flashed around him. **4** Falling to the ground, he heard a voice saying to him, "Saul, Saul, why are you persecuting Me?" **5** "Who are You, Lord?" he said. "I am Jesus, the One you are persecuting," He replied. **6** "But get up and go into the city, and you will be told what you must do." **7** The men who were traveling with him stood speechless, hearing the sound but seeing no one. **8** Then Saul got up from the ground, and though his eyes were open, he could see nothing. So they took him by the hand and led him into Damascus. **9** He was unable to see for three days and did not eat or drink.

15 The Lord said to [Ananias], "Go! For this man is My chosen instrument to take My name to Gentiles, kings, and the Israelites. **16** I will show him how much he must suffer for My name!" **17** So Ananias left and entered the house. Then he placed his hands on him and said, "Brother Saul, the Lord Jesus, who appeared to you on the road you were traveling, has sent me so that you can regain your sight and be filled with the Holy Spirit." **18** At once something like scales fell from his eyes, and he regained his sight. Then he got up and was baptized. **19** And after taking some food, he regained his strength. Saul was with the disciples in Damascus for some days. **20** Immediately he began proclaiming Jesus in the synagogues: "He is the Son of God."

❯ EXPLORE THE TEXT

THE CONFRONTATION *(Acts 9:3-6)*

³As [Saul] traveled and was nearing Damascus, a light from heaven suddenly flashed around him. ⁴Falling to the ground, he heard a voice saying to him, "Saul, Saul, why are you persecuting Me?" ⁵"Who are You, Lord?" he said. "I am Jesus, the One you are persecuting," He replied. ⁶"But get up and go into the city, and you will be told what you must do."

Saul was headed to Damascus, armed with arrest warrants for followers of Christ. Somewhere near the city, however, he was confronted by the risen Christ. The phrase "a light from heaven" (v. 3) indicated a divine intrusion. Later, when recounting his conversion experience to a king, Saul described the intensity of this light as "brighter than the sun" (26:13).

The flash of light was so intense that it forced Saul to fall to the ground, and he heard a voice that called him by name. Saul was suddenly confronted with the fact that to persecute Jesus' followers was to persecute the Son of God.

So far Saul was unsure of the speaker's identity, although his use of the term *Lord* suggests that he knew the voice was from God. What a stunning—and piercing—revelation it must have been to hear the divine voice. The same Lord Jesus to whom the dying martyr Stephen had prayed as Saul watched (see 7:58-59) was indeed alive and reigning in heaven!

A dramatic change came over Saul. A few minutes before, he was a self-righteous persecutor of Jesus. Then the risen Lord arrested Saul's heart, mind, and soul with a piercing flash of light. Now blinded, humbled, and prostrate in the dust, Saul received his first order from the One he had persecuted. Saul had a new life that would come with a new purpose. A former ungodly rebel was being transformed into a godly revolutionary.

How would you characterize the confrontation between Jesus and Saul? In what other ways does Jesus confront people about their need for Him?

THE COMPANIONS (Acts 9:7-9)

⁷The men who were traveling with him stood speechless, hearing the sound but seeing no one. ⁸Then Saul got up from the ground, and though his eyes were open, he could see nothing. So they took him by the hand and led him into Damascus. ⁹He was unable to see for three days and did not eat or drink.

Saul's traveling companions were affected by the encounter but in a different way than Saul was. First, they were speechless. They couldn't find the words to explain what happened, although they too had been knocked to the ground by the light along with Saul (see 26:14). Second, the men heard the sound that occurred but didn't recognize it as the voice of Jesus speaking to Saul (see 22:9). Third, the men saw no one. They were unaware of the Lord's presence, because either the Lord prevented them from seeing Him or they were spiritually unable to see.

Saul's traveling companions were prohibited from hearing Jesus' message to Saul. What does this detail teach us about the way God relates to His people?

Bewildered, broken, and powerless, Saul slowly rose to his feet in obedience to Jesus. The veil over his heart concerning Christ had been lifted, but his physical sight was yet to be restored. He could open his eyes, but he couldn't see anything. He stood helpless and dependent, no longer the proud, self-righteous Pharisee but rather the humbled follower of Christ who needed his companions to lead him by the hand into the city of Damascus.

Saul remained sightless for three days as he stayed in Damascus. He was also either fasting in repentance and meditation or was simply uninterested in food and drink in light of the dramatic changes in his life.

THE COMMISSION (Acts 9:15-20)

¹⁵The Lord said to [Ananias], "Go! For this man is My chosen instrument to take My name to Gentiles, kings, and the Israelites. ¹⁶I will show him how much he must suffer for My name!" ¹⁷So Ananias left and entered the house. Then he placed his hands on him and said, "Brother Saul, the Lord Jesus, who appeared to you on the road you were traveling, has sent me so that you can regain your sight and be filled with the Holy Spirit."

Many Christians quietly but effectively serve the Lord behind the scenes. Their names seldom appear in the news or in history books, but their obedience to God in crucial situations often shapes the future in remarkable ways. Such a believer was Ananias of Damascus, whom the Lord sent to instruct and baptize Saul. Ananias had heard about Saul's hostile activities against believers in Jerusalem and knew that Saul had come to Damascus with the same intent. He was hesitant to go and find Saul (see vv. 13-14), but the Lord explained that Saul was His chosen instrument to carry His message to "Gentiles, kings, and the Israelites" (v. 15).

Saul was well suited for the lifework God chose for him. He could communicate in Greek, Hebrew, and Aramaic. He was trained in the Old Testament Scriptures, was a citizen of the Roman Empire, and was able to support himself as a tent maker. But most significant of all, he had encountered the risen Lord and had been transformed.

BIBLE SKILL
Compare Bible verses to understand the writer's thoughts.

Compare Romans 1:1-5; 9:23-24; Galatians 1:15-16; and Ephesians 3:7-13. What do these passages reveal about Saul's (Paul's) understanding of his calling from God? What do these passages reveal about God and His work in the world? Summarize what you think Saul (Paul) understood that it meant for him to be a chosen instrument.

Saul's selection and suitability for the gospel mission also meant that Saul must suffer on behalf of Jesus. Those who walk closely in Jesus' steps can't avoid the burden of the cross or the pain of sacrifice. The verb "must suffer" (v 16) indicates a divine necessity. Saul would experience the agony and affliction of discipleship, yet he would never grow ashamed of his devotion to Christ (see 2 Tim. 1:12).

Ananias arrived at the place where Saul was staying. The Lord had previously given Ananias the exact house and address (see Acts 9:11). Moreover, in a vision Saul had already learned of the man's name who would come and restore his sight (see v. 12). How wonderful it must have felt when both men realized the Lord had been working in them to bring about His holy purpose!

Notice that Ananias addressed Saul tenderly as Brother Saul (see v. 17). Jews used the term *brother* as a word of courteous address; however, Christians came to use the term to indicate a spiritual relationship in the family of faith. Likewise, Ananias's placing his hands on Saul demonstrated the bond the Holy Spirit created in the family of God. Ananias had come to Saul in the Lord's authority to restore Saul's sight and to pray so that Saul could be filled with the Holy Spirit.

Bible students sometimes debate the precise time when Saul was saved. Some hold that it happened on the Damascus road. Others suggest that it occurred during the three-day period in Damascus (see vv. 9-11). Still others propose that Saul's conversion happened during Ananias's visit. What we can know with absolute certainty is that Jesus saved and changed Saul, forgiving him of his sin. The Holy Spirit filled Saul and began to prepare him for the great work of taking the gospel to the ends of the earth.

How important is it for a believer to be able to pinpoint the precise time of his or her conversion? Explain.

18At once something like scales fell from his eyes, and he regained his sight. Then he got up and was baptized. **19**And after taking some food, he regained his strength. Saul was with the disciples in Damascus for some days. **20**Immediately he began proclaiming Jesus in the synagogues: "He is the Son of God."

As Ananias conveyed Jesus' promise, Saul regained his sight. The Greek term for *scales* was used to refer to anything from an onion peel to fish scales to snowflakes. The text simply says that what fell off Saul's eyes resembled scales.

Next Saul got up and was baptized. Saul's baptism was an act of obedience and Saul's public profession of being a follower of Jesus Christ. Saul's baptism signaled the end of his fasting. He regained his strength to go along with his restored eyesight. Equally important, he gained spiritual strength by meeting for several days with the disciples in Damascus.

No doubt many of the Jews who heard Saul proclaim Jesus wondered how a fervent-hearted Pharisee's message could change so radically. Saul preached Jesus as the Son of God, a title that affirmed Jesus as Deity and as the long-awaited Messiah of Israel.

Why was it significant that Saul immediately began to proclaim Jesus? Why do new believers often display passion for telling others about Jesus?

❯ OBEY THE TEXT

God uses all kinds of people in kingdom work and does so in different ways. God calls specific individuals to focus on mission work. All believers can share with others who Jesus is.

Share your conversion experience with someone in your group. In what ways did your conversion differ from Saul's conversion? In what ways was it similar?

Ask God to help you understand your role in His mission. Thank Him for ways He has used you in the past. Commit to be available to Him in the future. Ask God to call people in your group to share the gospel with people who have yet to hear His truth.

Record your understanding of who Jesus is. Name one person with whom you can share what you have recorded. Ask God to help you share with this person in the next week.

MEMORIZE

"Immediately he began proclaiming Jesus in the synagogues: "He is the Son of God." Acts 9:20

USE THE SPACE PROVIDED TO MAKE OBSERVATIONS AND RECORD PRAYER
REQUESTS DURING THE GROUP EXPERIENCE FOR THIS SESSION.

MY THOUGHTS

Record insights and questions from the group experience.

MY RESPONSE

Note specific ways you'll put into practice the truth explored this week.

MY PRAYERS

List specific prayer needs and answers to remember this week.

SALVATION IS FOR EVERYONE

The gospel message is meant for every person of every background, life experience, and heritage.

UNDERSTAND THE CONTEXT

USE THE FOLLOWING PAGES TO PREPARE FOR YOUR GROUP TIME.

Luke continued to follow the apostle Peter's evangelistic work. Having seen widespread response to the gospel in Joppa following the raising of Tabitha from the dead, Peter remained there. Peter would soon receive a visit from three men of a nearby city; their urgent request would bring about a transformation in Peter's attitude toward Gentiles.

Luke first described the situation of Cornelius, a devoutly religious Gentile centurion living in Caesarea. In a time of prayer, Cornelius had a vision in which an angel of God instructed him to send to Joppa for Peter. Cornelius sent two servants and a soldier to ask the apostle to come to Caesarea (see Acts 10:1-8).

Meanwhile, Peter also received a vision during a time of prayer. The meaning of his vision became clear to Peter as he met the three visitors from Caesarea, went with them to Cornelius's house, and heard Cornelius's testimony about the angel's instructions to send for the apostle. Peter was to explain the gospel to them (see vv. 17-43). As Peter preached, the Holy Spirit came on Cornelius and the others gathered in his house. Peter then instructed the new believers to be baptized (see vv. 44-48).

Luke then reported Peter's return to Jerusalem. There Peter was confronted by some Jewish Christians who were offended that he had not only visited but had also eaten with Gentiles. Peter explained everything that had led to his stay with Cornelius and emphasized that the Gentiles had received the Holy Spirit just as Jewish converts had. This was a breakthrough revelation for the early church (11:1-18).

In 11:19–12:25 Luke described how despite opposition, the gospel spread from Jerusalem into places such as Antioch of Syria. The church in Antioch would play a key role both in the life of Saul of Tarsus and in the spread of the gospel to all nations. It was also in Antioch that followers of Jesus first came to be known as Christians.

"IF YOU TAKE MISSIONS OUT OF THE BIBLE, YOU WON'T HAVE ANYTHING LEFT BUT THE COVERS."

—Nina Gunter

⟩ ACTS 10:9-16,43-48

Think About It

Notice Peter's reaction to the vision. How would you characterize his reaction?

What does the question Peter asked in verse 47 indicate about his further response to the vision?

9 The next day, as they were traveling and nearing the city, Peter went up to pray on the housetop about noon. **10** Then he became hungry and wanted to eat, but while they were preparing something, he went into a visionary state. **11** He saw heaven opened and an object that resembled a large sheet coming down, being lowered by its four corners to the earth. **12** In it were all the four-footed animals and reptiles of the earth, and the birds of the sky. **13** Then a voice said to him, "Get up, Peter; kill and eat!" **14** "No, Lord!" Peter said. "For I have never eaten anything common and ritually unclean!" **15** Again, a second time, a voice said to him, "What God has made clean, you must not call common." **16** This happened three times, and then the object was taken up into heaven.

43 "All the prophets testify about Him that through His name everyone who believes in Him will receive forgiveness of sins." **44** While Peter was still speaking these words, the Holy Spirit came down on all those who heard the message. **45** The circumcised believers who had come with Peter were astounded because the gift of the Holy Spirit had been poured out on the Gentiles also. **46** For they heard them speaking in other languages and declaring the greatness of God. Then Peter responded, **47** "Can anyone withhold water and prevent these people from being baptized, who have received the Holy Spirit just as we have?" **48** And he commanded them to be baptized in the name of Jesus Christ. Then they asked him to stay for a few days.

❯ EXPLORE THE TEXT

THE VISIONS *(Acts 10:9-16)*

⁹**The next day, as they were traveling and nearing the city, Peter went up to pray on the housetop about noon. ¹⁰Then he became hungry and wanted to eat, but while they were preparing something, he went into a visionary state.**

The phrase "the next day" (v. 9) refers to the day after Cornelius, the Roman governor, had his vision in Caesarea and sent three representatives to Joppa to find Peter (see vv. 3-8). Caesarea, located on the Mediterranean coast about 35 miles north of Joppa, served as the capital of Judea. Its population was a mix of Jews and Gentiles, but the two groups didn't always live together peacefully. Cornelius, however, maintained a good relationship with the Jewish population and may have been recognized by the Jews as a God fearer (see v. 2).

Meanwhile, Peter was still a guest in the home of Simon the tanner in Joppa (see 9:43). Around noontime Peter went up to the roof of the house to pray. Thus, God prepared the hearts of both Cornelius and Peter while they were praying.

The fact that Peter became hungry prepares readers for the vision to come. Peter was about to learn that Jews were not the only people who hungered to know God. More important, he was about to learn that the gospel is life-giving "food" bestowed by God on Jews and Gentiles alike.

Peter would initially be confronted with this truth in a visionary state, which is a profound spiritual experience dictated by divine activity. God brought this vision on Peter to prepare him for his upcoming visit to Cornelius's house.

[11]He saw heaven opened and an object that resembled a large sheet coming down, being lowered by its four corners to the earth. [12]In it were all the four-footed animals and reptiles of the earth, and the birds of the sky. [13]Then a voice said to him, "Get up, Peter; kill and eat!" [14]"No, Lord!" Peter said. "For I have never eaten anything common and ritually unclean!" [15]Again, a second time, a voice said to him, "What God has made clean, you must not call common." [16]This happened three times, and then the object was taken up into heaven.

In his vision Peter saw an object that resembled a large sheet being lowered from heaven by its four corners. The object served as an enormous pouch that contained all types of creatures. The law of Moses strictly distinguished between clean and unclean creatures (see Lev. 11). Unclean creatures were not to be eaten or even handled; violators of these rules would be deemed unholy before God. Therefore, many Jews viewed all Gentiles as being detestable before God because they didn't keep the law. What possible message could Peter gain from a vision of both clean and unclean creatures in one large pouch?

Suddenly Peter heard a voice instructing him to eat. (Recall that Peter was hungry.) No caveat followed the command; Peter could feast on any creature he desired. But as suddenly and emphatically as the divine voice gave permission, Peter answered, "No, Lord!" (Acts 10:14). Ironically, the "wall" erected by the law that forbade Peter from eating anything common and ritually unclean now hindered the apostle from gratefully saying yes to God's gift of food.

Peter's reaction carries far-reaching implications for believers today. In what areas of our lives are we saying no to God? When we say no to God, we disobey His authority. Moreover, we deny ourselves many wonderful blessings He wants to give us and spiritual truths He wants to teach us.

Think of other examples in Scripture when people said no to God. How do those examples compare with Peter's response?

Repetition is a valuable teaching-learning method. Peter experienced either part or all of the vision three times (see v. 16). After the second time, the voice delivered the gospel principle that would shatter Peter's "wall" of tradition: "What God has made clean, you must not call common" (v. 15). Peter would soon apply the principle in real life, proclaiming at Cornelius's house that Jesus' atoning death on the cross makes clean (saves) anyone who repents and believes in Him, whether Jew or Gentile.

In what way could the early church have been affected if God had allowed Peter to dismiss the heavenly vision?

THE DECLARATION (Acts 10:43)

⁴³"All the prophets testify about Him that through His name everyone who believes in Him will receive forgiveness of sins."

At this point we have fast-forwarded through the narrative that describes the arrival of Cornelius's messengers in Joppa (see v. 17), their urgent invitation for Peter to come to Caesarea and preach the gospel at Cornelius's house (see v. 22), Peter's agreement to go (see v. 23), and the apostle's message to the people gathered at Cornelius's house (see vv. 34-43). Verse 43 is a key statement in Peter's message; it prompted a movement of the Holy Spirit among the hearers.

With the phrase "all the prophets" (v. 43) Peter declared that the prior testimony of the Old Testament foretold the truth about Jesus. The prophet Isaiah declared that the Messiah would bear the sin of humanity and "justify many" (Isa. 53:11). The prophet Zechariah asserted that the Messiah would release a cleansing spiritual fountain to wash away impurities (see Zech. 13:1). The prophet Malachi predicted that the Messiah would bring healing in His wings to all who revered His name (see Mal. 4:2).

Peter continued to learn the significance of his vision. Read Galatians 2:11-16. What does this event reveal about the difficulty of overcoming social barriers? How did God use Paul to reinforce to Peter (Cephas) the truth of Peter's vision in Acts 10:9-16? What does this exchange between Paul and Peter teach us about the need to be reminded of truths that God has revealed to us in the past?

What other Bible passages can you identify that support Peter's declaration of salvation for all who repent and believe in Jesus?

THE SIGN *(Acts 10:44-46a)*

⁴⁴While Peter was still speaking these words, the Holy Spirit came down on all those who heard the message. ⁴⁵The circumcised believers who had come with Peter were astounded because the gift of the Holy Spirit had been poured out on the Gentiles also. ⁴⁶For they heard them speaking in other languages and declaring the greatness of God.

The Holy Spirit's ability to break through to listeners is always greater than a gospel witness's ability to communicate. Still, the Spirit used Peter's words as fuel to ignite a fire in the hearers' hearts. The Spirit descended on Cornelius and the others while Peter was still speaking. Their hearts were ready and open to believe in Jesus. The phrase "circumcised believers" (v. 45) refers to the Jewish Christians from Joppa who went with Peter to Caesarea (see v. 23). They were astounded when they saw the outpouring of the Holy Spirit on Gentiles. They witnessed clear evidence that the gospel welcomes all people into God's family by faith in Jesus Christ.

There are similarities between this event in Caesarea and the outpouring of the Spirit in Jerusalem on the Day of Pentecost. Both events were solely initiated by the Holy Spirit to magnify Jesus as God's Son. At both events the Spirit came down on all who believed. Likewise, at both events the Spirit gave believers the ability to speak in other languages than their own in order to declare the greatness of God. God confirmed the Gentiles' salvation by faith in Christ in the same way that He confirmed the salvation of Jewish believers on the Day of Pentecost (see 2:1-4). This was a pivotal event in the movement of the gospel toward global impact as the Holy Spirit opened the door of hope for every tribe, race, and nation.

THE ACCEPTANCE *(Acts 10:46b-48)*

⁴⁶Then Peter responded, ⁴⁷"Can anyone withhold water and prevent these people from being baptized, who have received the Holy Spirit just as we have?" ⁴⁸And he commanded them to be baptized in the name of Jesus Christ. Then they asked him to stay for a few days.

If the Holy Spirit gave to the Gentiles the same indwelling blessing that He gave to the Jews, then it meant God in Christ had purified Cornelius and his household and had made them pleasing in His sight. For Peter, therefore, the next step for these new believers was clear. Peter thus directed Cornelius and the other Gentiles to be baptized in the name of Jesus Christ. Baptism is a public demonstration of submission to Jesus as Savior and Lord. Immersion into water has no saving power in and of itself. That's why the new converts were to be baptized in the name of Jesus Christ. He is the One who saves and cleanses His followers from their sins.

Peter's command was met by an enthusiastic reception. Moreover, these new believers displayed a spiritual hunger to hear even more about Jesus and their new life in Him. Perhaps they also thought about other friends and neighbors who needed to hear the gospel. In any case they urged Peter to stay in Caesarea for a few days.

How would you describe the significance of the Gentile believers' baptism to the Jewish believers present? To other Gentiles present?

❯ OBEY THE TEXT

Salvation is offered to all, regardless of heritage or race. Salvation comes through faith in Jesus alone. Believers can be advocates in the local church for new believers from different backgrounds.

What social barriers cause you the greatest difficulties? How do those barriers affect your ability or willingness to witness to people in those groups? What actions can you take to remove those barriers?

Consider your salvation. What evidence could you point to that demonstrates that you're trusting Christ alone for your salvation?

What activities will you and your Bible-study group initiate to be more inclusive of people outside your church? Identify barriers that need to be torn down and initiate a plan for addressing those barriers.

MEMORIZE

"Peter began to speak: 'Now I really understand that God doesn't show favoritism.' " Acts 10:34

USE THE SPACE PROVIDED TO MAKE OBSERVATIONS AND RECORD PRAYER
REQUESTS DURING THE GROUP EXPERIENCE FOR THIS SESSION.

MY THOUGHTS

Record insights and questions from the group experience.

MY RESPONSE

Note specific ways you'll put into practice the truth explored this week.

MY PRAYERS

List specific prayer needs and answers to remember this week.

❯ GETTING STARTED

OPENING OPTIONS: Choose one of the following to open the group discussion.

WEEKLY QUOTATION DISCUSSION STARTER: "We talk of the Second Coming; half the world has never heard of the first."—Oswald J. Smith

> ❯ What's your initial response to this week's quotation?

> ❯ How often do you think about Jesus' return?

> ❯ How often do you consider the existence of people who've never heard the gospel?

> ❯ Does Jesus' return seem to be a topic of debate among Christians or a daily reality? Explain.

> ❯ Today we'll see Jesus' earthly presence coming to an end and the promise of His return.

CREATIVE ACTIVITY: To prepare, identify a time when you were surprised. If possible, secure a picture or another object that reminds you of or represents that memory. When everyone has arrived, open your time together by briefly sharing this surprising experience. Then use the following to open the discussion.

> ❯ When have you been completely surprised? Why were you surprised?

> ❯ Today we'll read about something Jesus said and did that was completely unexpected.

❯ UNDERSTAND THE CONTEXT

PROVIDE BACKGROUND: Briefly introduce members to the Book of Acts by pointing out the major themes and any information or ideas that will help them understand Acts 1 (see pp. 7 and 9). Then, to help people personally connect today's context with the original context, use the following questions and statements.

> ❯ Luke authored two books. The Gospel of Luke focused on the birth, life, death, and resurrection of Jesus. The Book of Acts focused on the spread of the gospel and establishment of the church after Jesus' ascension into heaven. Why would both books have been important for the original audience? Why are they still important for readers today?

> ❯ As we begin our study of the Book of Acts, pay attention to the different ways God worked to spread the gospel of Jesus.

❯ EXPLORE THE TEXT

READ THE BIBLE: Ask a volunteer to read Acts 1:1-11.

DISCUSS: Use the following questions to discuss group members' initial reactions to the text.

› How do you understand the word *began* in the phrase "all that Jesus began to do and teach" in verse 1?

› Why are the first two verses foundational to an understanding of the rest of the Book of Acts?

› Why is it important that verse 3 establishes Jesus' resurrection as proven historical fact?

› What key points in verse 3 provide a summation of the gospel introduced in verses 1-2?

› What was promised in verses 4-5? Why were the disciples told to wait rather than immediately spread the good news of Jesus and the kingdom of God?

› In verses 6-8 why is it significant that Jesus said the power of the Holy Spirit was necessary for the disciples' mission, but knowledge of God's timing wasn't possible?

› Why would being witnesses throughout the earth be of greater importance than seeking a kingdom in Israel?

› Why did the Book of Acts open with Jesus' ascension and a promise that He would return?

› What does this Scripture passage reveal about God's character? About natural human tendencies? About our mission as Christians?

NOTE: Provide ample time for group members to share responses and questions about the text. Don't feel pressured to prioritize the printed agenda over group members' personal experiences. If time allows, discuss responses to the questions in the personal reading.

❯ OBEY THE TEXT

RESPOND: Foster an environment of openness and action. Help individuals apply biblical truth to specific areas of personal thought, attitude, and/or behavior.

› How do you feel knowing that even the disciples still didn't fully understand what Jesus was doing? Why are you encouraged or discouraged that Jesus said we'll never know God's timing?

› In what ways can we encourage one another to go in obedience to Jesus instead of delaying or doing nothing?

› How are you currently seeking to obey Jesus' final words to be His witness?

PRAY: Close by thanking God for Jesus. Pray for hearts that are eager to share the good news of Jesus and the hope we have in His return.

❯ GETTING STARTED

OPENING OPTIONS: Choose one of the following to open the group discussion.

WEEKLY QUOTATION DISCUSSION STARTER: "God's work done in God's way will never lack God's supply."—Hudson Taylor

> ❯ What's your initial response to this week's quotation?

> ❯ When have you experienced God's provision? How was it related to His purpose?

> ❯ Today we'll see the most important way God provides for the work He commissioned.

CREATIVE ACTIVITY: To prepare, identify a team, band, club, organization, or fraternity/sorority to which you belonged. This could be a meaningful experience to inspire your group or an embarrassing moment that's funny and reveals personal humility and openness to the people in your group. If you have an object from that season of your life, be prepared to show it to your group. When everyone has arrived, open your time together by briefly sharing your story. Then use the following to open the discussion.

> ❯ When have you been part of a team, band, club, organization, or fraternity/sorority?

> ❯ What type of group was it, and what was your purpose for joining?

> ❯ Did the group fulfill your expectations? Why or why not?

> ❯ Today we'll look at the way God formed a new community of people around His great purpose.

❯ UNDERSTAND THE CONTEXT

PROVIDE BACKGROUND: Briefly introduce members to major themes, information, and ideas that will help them understand Acts 2 (see p. 17). Then, to help people personally connect today's context with the original context, use the following questions and statements.

> ❯ Why would it have been important for early Christians to understand the origin of the church?

> ❯ What's the perceived role of the church in today's culture?

> ❯ In today's study look for key events and characteristics of the early church.

❯ EXPLORE THE TEXT

READ THE BIBLE: Ask two volunteers to read Acts 2:1-4,41-47.

DISCUSS: Use the following questions to discuss group members' initial reactions to the text.

> In verses 1-4 why was the Holy Spirit given while people were gathered together? Why is it significant that the Spirit appeared to, rested on, and filled each of them? What's the importance of the fact that the presence and power of the Holy Spirit were given before the public preaching of the gospel and formation of the church in Jerusalem?

> In verse 41 how did three thousand people respond to Peter's first Spirit-filled sermon? Why was each of these details recorded in this text?

> To what things were the earliest believers in Jesus devoted? Why is each of the things described in verses 41-42 essential to the Christian life and to a healthy church?

> Why is the word *through* the key to understanding the event described in verse 43? Why did fear come over people at the sudden, miraculous beginning of the church?

> Verses 44-47 describe regular occurrences in the life of the church. What did the people do? What did God do?

> What does this Scripture passage reveal about God's character? About natural human tendencies? About our mission as Christians?

NOTE: Provide ample time for group members to share responses and questions about the text. Don't feel pressured to prioritize the printed agenda over group members' personal experiences. If time allows, discuss responses to the questions in the personal reading.

❯ OBEY THE TEXT

RESPOND: Foster an environment of openness and action. Help individuals apply biblical truth to specific areas of personal thought, attitude, and/or behavior.

> Could you be described as joyful, humble, generous, and devoted? Which characteristic of the early believers would be hardest for people to recognize in you?

> In what ways does your church resemble the description in Acts 2? In what areas can you help your church and your group draw people to Jesus?

> How are you encouraged in your daily life by meeting publicly in the church and personally in this group?

PRAY: Close by praising God for salvation. Pray for devotion to and health in your church.

❯ GETTING STARTED

OPENING OPTIONS: Choose one of the following to open the group discussion.

WEEKLY QUOTATION DISCUSSION STARTER: "I want to invest my life in something that is going to outlive me."—Vance H. Pitman

> ❯ What's your initial response to this week's quotation?

> ❯ Culturally, would you say our society as a whole lives for the moment, or do you see a secular desire to invest in a greater good? Explain your answer.

> ❯ What does it look like to invest our lives as Christians in something greater than ourselves?

> ❯ Today we'll see how the early Christians invested their lives in something more than themselves.

CREATIVE ACTIVITY: To prepare, secure a prized possession, one you'd do almost anything to keep or went to great lengths to obtain. If it's not an object but an experience or a relationship, be prepared to tell that story and share any visual representation. When everyone has arrived, open the session by telling your story. Then use the following to open the discussion.

> ❯ Explain that most of us have something we are or have been willing to do anything necessary to obtain or keep.

> ❯ Has there ever been anything you wanted so badly that you laid everything on the line, no matter the personal cost (reputation, cost, etc.) to obtain it? Was it worth it?

> ❯ Today we'll see people who were willing to lay it all on the line, even their lives.

❯ UNDERSTAND THE CONTEXT

PROVIDE BACKGROUND: Briefly introduce members to major themes, information, and ideas that will help them understand Acts 5 (see p. 27). Then, to help people personally connect today's context with the original context, use the following questions and statements.

> ❯ Why was it important for the original audience to be aware of persecution? Why is it still important for readers today?

> ❯ In what ways is being a Christian countercultural today?

> ❯ In today's study pay attention to the response of both the persecuted and the persecutors.

❯ EXPLORE THE TEXT

READ THE BIBLE: Ask three volunteers to read Acts 5:21,25-35,38-42.

DISCUSS: Use the following questions to discuss group members' initial reactions to the text.

> In verse 25 how did God affirm His power? How was this demonstration of power related to His mission?

> In verses 26-28 why did the religious leaders want to silence the gospel?

> How would you describe the nature of Peter's declaration in verse 29? Why was Peter confident? How do Peter's declaration and attitude contrast with that of the Sanhedrin?

> What key points in Peter's response, in verses 29-32, summarized the gospel? How was his gospel presentation both convicting and encouraging?

> In verses 33-39 in what ways was Gamaliel's advice both practical and prophetic?

> How did the apostles respond to unjust, abusive treatment? Review every response in today's Scripture verses.

> What made the apostles' response of faithfulness and rejoicing possible?

> What does this Scripture passage reveal about God's character? About natural human tendencies? About our mission as Christians?

NOTE: Provide ample time for group members to share responses and questions about the text. Don't feel pressured to prioritize the printed agenda over group members' personal experiences. If time allows, discuss responses to the questions in the personal reading.

❯ OBEY THE TEXT

RESPOND: Foster an environment of openness and action. Help individuals apply biblical truth to specific areas of personal thought, attitude, and/or behavior.

> When have you experienced consequences for expressing your faith?

> How would you feel if you faced severe persecution in our culture? What would it take for you to remain devoted to your faith? To spreading the gospel?

> How can you boldly share the good news of Jesus this week, even if a witness would be unpopular or if you would face personal consequences?

PRAY: Close by praising God for the infinite value of knowing Him through faith in Jesus. Ask His Spirit to strengthen every member's faith and confidence in the face of opposition or difficulty.

❯ GETTING STARTED

OPENING OPTIONS: Choose one of the following to open the group discussion.

WEEKLY QUOTATION DISCUSSION STARTER: "Sympathy is no substitute for action."
—David Livingstone

> ❯ What's your initial response to this week's quotation?

> ❯ How has technology raised awareness of genuine needs? How has technology potentially led to passivity? In what ways are awareness and action different?

> ❯ About what issues do you see many people expressing strong opinions, perhaps especially on social media, but few people actually taking action to address the cause?

> ❯ Today we'll see that the Spirit moves not only to make people aware of issues but also to spur them to action.

CREATIVE ACTIVITY: To prepare, find and bring a ball or another object that can tossed around your group. When everyone has arrived, open by playing a game in which everyone spontaneously tosses the item from person to person in random order. The object is to see how many times group members can touch the object without dropping it. After the game use the following to open your discussion.

> ❯ What was the hardest part of this game?

> ❯ Who had the quickest reaction time?

> ❯ Today we'll see that readiness is needed to react to opportunities presented by the Spirit.

❯ UNDERSTAND THE CONTEXT

PROVIDE BACKGROUND: Briefly introduce members to major themes, information, and ideas that will help them understand Acts 8 (see p. 37). Then, to help people personally connect today's context with the original context, use the following questions and statements.

> ❯ Why was it important for the original audience to see how people outside Jerusalem began responding to the gospel? Why is it still important for readers today to see these responses?

> ❯ In our society certain jobs require constant vigilance. For example, firefighters need not only to be made aware of needs but also to respond quickly to what may be a life-or-death situation.

> ❯ In today's study pay attention to people's responses to immediate circumstances that resulted in eternal life instead of death.

❯ EXPLORE THE TEXT

READ THE BIBLE: Ask a volunteer to read Acts 8:26-39.

DISCUSS: Use the following questions to discuss group members' initial reactions to the text.

› What details make verses 26-28 interesting parts of the story rather than a simple list of background facts? How do theses verses reveal a specific plan of God rather than random chance and coincidence?

› In verses 29-35 how does Scripture play an important role in the conversation? How does this account prove that all Scripture, even the Old Testament, centers on the good news of Jesus?

› In verses 36-39 why does the water have physical significance? Why does the water have spiritual significance? What do the Ethiopian's question and action reveal about baptism?

› How did Philip respond to each prompt from God? How did he respond to the Ethiopian?

› How did the Ethiopian respond to Philip? What parts of the conversation and actions are surprising? Why are these elements surprising?

› What does this Scripture passage reveal about God's character? About natural human tendencies? About our mission as Christians?

NOTE: Provide ample time for group members to share responses and questions about the text. Don't feel pressured to prioritize the printed agenda over group members' personal experiences. If time allows, discuss responses to the questions in the personal reading.

❯ OBEY THE TEXT

RESPOND: Foster an environment of openness and action. Help individuals apply biblical truth to specific areas of personal thought, attitude, and/or behavior.

› Who shared the gospel with you? What was the situation, and what was your response?

› How often do you take the opportunity to talk to someone about your faith? When was the most recent time you shared the gospel? Describe what you felt before, during, and after?

› Whom has God brought into your life who needs help to grow in his or her understanding of Scripture? What will you do to help him or her?

› With what individuals do you cross paths on a regular basis who don't yet believe the gospel? How can you intentionally make yourself available to the Spirit's work in their lives?

PRAY: Close by thanking God for bringing the good news of Jesus to each person in your group. Ask for a discerning, obedient heart to eagerly share the gospel with others at any time.

❯ GETTING STARTED

OPENING OPTIONS: Choose one of the following to open the group discussion.

WEEKLY QUOTATION DISCUSSION STARTER: "The gospel is only good news if it gets there in time." —Carl F. H. Henry

> ❯ What's your initial response to this week's quotation?

> ❯ When have you missed out on something exciting because you didn't know about it or were too late? How did you feel?

> ❯ Today we'll see that God wants everyone to hear the gospel.

CREATIVE ACTIVITY: To prepare, get a sheet of paper for everyone in the group. When everyone has arrived, open your time together by passing out the paper and instructing everyone to transform their sheets of paper into shapes that can fly across the room. After a minute prompt people individually or simultaneously to throw their paper away from where they're sitting. Then use the following to open the discussion.

> ❯ How did you choose what to do with your paper?

> ❯ Did your design accomplish the purpose?

> ❯ Today we'll see that God has a specific purpose in transforming people's lives.

❯ UNDERSTAND THE CONTEXT

PROVIDE BACKGROUND: Briefly introduce members to major themes, information, and ideas that will help them understand Acts 9 (see p. 47). Then, to help people personally connect today's context with the original context, use the following questions and statements.

> ❯ Why was it important for the original audience to know stories of radical transformation? Why was the story of Saul, a devout Jewish man "breathing threats and murder against the disciples" (v. 1) of particular importance? Why are these accounts still important for readers today?

> ❯ Historically or in recent news, how have misguided Christians acted contrary to Jesus' mission of spreading the gospel to all people?

> ❯ As we begin today's study, pray that the Holy Spirit will open your eyes to areas of misunderstanding, self-righteousness, or sin to which you're blind.

❯ EXPLORE THE TEXT

READ THE BIBLE: Ask two volunteers to read Acts 9:3-9,15-20.

DISCUSS: Use the following questions to discuss group members' initial reactions to the text.

> In verses 3-5 why is it significant that Jesus said Saul was persecuting Him? Why is it significant that Jesus identified Saul by name? What do these facts reveal about a relationship with Jesus?

> In verses 6-9 what details emphasize the radical yet personal nature of conversion?

> What did Ananias's response to the Lord reveal in spite of his fear of Saul's reputation (see vv. 15-19)?

> What verses speak of God's plan for individual salvation? God's plan for all nations?

> Why was suffering part of the message for Saul in verse 16?

> What specific actions reveal true repentance and transformation in the life of Saul?

> What does this Scripture passage reveal about God's character? About natural human tendencies? About our mission as Christians?

NOTE: Provide ample time for group members to share responses and questions about the text. Don't feel pressured to prioritize the printed agenda over group members' personal experiences. If time allows, discuss responses to the questions in the personal reading.

❯ OBEY THE TEXT

RESPOND: Foster an environment of openness and action. Help individuals apply biblical truth to specific areas of personal thought, attitude, and/or behavior.

> In your religious devotion how have you ever looked down on or acted hatefully toward others?

> Like Saul, when have you realized you were wrong about something you once considered to be right in God's eyes?

> Would anyone say certain people would be surprised to know you're a Christian today? Why would it be surprising?

> How has Jesus changed your life?

> Like Ananias, how can you reach out and encourage someone else in his or her Christian faith?

PRAY: Close by praying for humility before God and other people. Ask for an openness to be corrected in places where we're wrong or self-righteous. Thank God for His grace and the life-changing power of His Spirit in the lives of everyone in your group and around the world.

❯ GETTING STARTED

OPENING OPTIONS: Choose one of the following to open the group discussion.

WEEKLY QUOTATION DISCUSSION STARTER: "If you take missions out of the Bible, you won't have anything left but the covers."—Nina Gunter

> ❯ What's your initial response to this week's quotation?

> ❯ In your own words, what's the Bible? Why do we have the Bible?

> ❯ How would you explain to someone the message of the Bible?

> ❯ Today we'll see why we can say every page of Scripture tells a story of God's seeking, saving, and setting people apart as He makes Himself known to the world.

CREATIVE ACTIVITY: To prepare, secure a highlighter and a map of the world (you may need to print a map). Identify the farthest place to which you've traveled. When everyone has arrived, open your time together by briefly sharing a story of where you traveled and why, highlighting the location on your map. Then use the following to open the discussion.

> ❯ What's the farthest you've traveled? Highlight on the map each destination members identify.

> ❯ Why did you travel to this destination?

> ❯ Today we'll see how God continued to take the good news of Jesus and the powerful presence of the Holy Spirit to new places in order to include all people of all cultures.

❯ UNDERSTAND THE CONTEXT

PROVIDE BACKGROUND: Briefly introduce members to major themes, information, and ideas that will help them understand Acts 10–12 (see p. 57). Then, to help people personally connect today's context with the original context, use the following questions and statements.

> ❯ Why was it important for the original audience to see a story of prejudice? Why is it still important for readers today?

> ❯ As we begin today's study, pay attention to excuses justifying prejudice and the way they were overcome.

❯ EXPLORE THE TEXT

READ THE BIBLE: Ask two volunteers to read Acts 10:9-16,43-48.

DISCUSS: Use the following questions to discuss group members' initial reactions to the text.

> What details in verses 9-10 remind us that Peter was an ordinary follower of Christ? Why are seemingly mundane or routine details important when recorded in Scripture?

> How did the vision in verses 11-16 symbolize God's breaking down barriers to include every culture as equal in His eyes? What did Peter's response reveal? What did God's response reveal?

> How do verses 44-48 resemble what we studied about the beginning of the church in Acts 2:1-4,41)? Why did God again reveal the Holy Spirit in this way to these people?

> What's the significance of baptism in this passage? How is it consistent with the role of baptism in the other texts we studied in previous sessions?

> How would you summarize this text? How would you summarize the theme of Acts 1–12?

> What does this Scripture passage reveal about God's character? About natural human tendencies? About our mission as Christians?

NOTE: Provide ample time for group members to share responses and questions about the text. Don't feel pressured to prioritize the printed agenda over group members' personal experiences. If time allows, discuss responses to the questions in the personal reading.

❯ OBEY THE TEXT

RESPOND: Foster an environment of openness and action. Help individuals apply biblical truth to specific areas of personal thought, attitude, and/or behavior.

> Is there anyone in your life with whom you intentionally don't share the gospel? If so, why?

> Is there any person or group of people you honestly feel will never believe in Jesus as Lord and Savior? Why not?

> How does today's text encourage or convict you about your attitude and actions in regard to sharing the gospel with others?

> What will you do in response to our study of Acts to share the gospel with all people?

PRAY: Close by thanking God for spreading the gospel and giving His Spirit to all people, including you. Pray for a heart of conviction to share the good news of Jesus with your family, friends, and people around you, even in places you've never considered. Ask for openness to go wherever, do whatever, and say whatever the Spirit prompts you for the sake His mission.

❯ TIPS FOR LEADING A GROUP

PRAYERFULLY PREPARE

Prepare for each session by—

> **reviewing the weekly material and group questions ahead of time;**

> **praying for each person in the group.**

Ask the Holy Spirit to work through you and the group discussion to help people take steps toward Jesus each week as directed by God's Word.

MINIMIZE DISTRACTIONS

Create a comfortable environment. If group members are uncomfortable, they'll be distracted and therefore not engaged in the group experience. Plan ahead by taking into consideration—

> **seating;**

> **temperature;**

> **lighting;**

> **food or drink;**

> **surrounding noise;**

> **general cleanliness (put pets away if meeting in a home).**

At best, thoughtfulness and hospitality show guests and group members they're welcome and valued in whatever environment you choose to gather. At worst, people may never notice your effort, but they're also not distracted. Do everything in your ability to help people focus on what's most important: connecting with God, with the Bible, and with others.

INCLUDE OTHERS

Your goal is to foster a community in which people are welcome just as they are but encouraged to grow spiritually. Always be aware of opportunities to—

> **invite** new people to join your group;

> **include** any people who visit the group.

An inexpensive way to make first-time guests feel welcome or to invite people to get involved is to give them their own copies of this Bible-study book.

ENCOURAGE DISCUSSION

A good small group has the following characteristics.

> **Everyone participates.** Encourage everyone to ask questions, share responses, or read aloud.

> **No one dominates—not even the leader.** Be sure what you say takes up less than half of your time together as a group. Politely redirect discussion if anyone dominates.

> **Nobody is rushed through questions.** Don't feel that a moment of silence is a bad thing. People often need time to think about their responses to questions they've just heard or to gain courage to share what God is stirring in their hearts.

> **Input is affirmed and followed up.** Make sure you point out something true or helpful in a response. Don't just move on. Build personal connections with follow-up questions, asking how other people have experienced similar things or how a truth has shaped their understanding of God and the Scripture you're studying. People are less likely to speak up if they fear that you don't actually want to hear their answers or that you're looking for only a certain answer.

> **God and His Word are central.** Opinions and experiences can be helpful, but God has given us the truth. Trust Scripture to be the authority and God's Spirit to work in people's lives. You can't change anyone, but God can. Continually point people to the Word and to active steps of faith.

KEEP CONNECTING

Think of ways to connect with members during the week. Participation during the session is always improved when members spend time connecting with one another away from the session. The more people are comfortable with and involved in one another's lives, the more they'll look forward to being together. When people move beyond being friendly and in the same group to truly being friends who form a community, they come to each session eager to engage instead of merely attending.

Encourage group members with thoughts, commitments, or questions from the session by connecting through—

> emails;
> texts;
> social media.

When possible, build deeper friendships by planning or spontaneously inviting group members to join you outside your regularly scheduled group time for—

> meals;
> fun activities;
> projects around your home, church, or community.

❯ GROUP CONTACT INFORMATION

Name _____ Number _____
Email/social media _____

Name _____ Number _____
Email/social media _____

Name _____ Number _____
Email/social media _____

Name _____ Number _____
Email/social media _____

Name _____ Number _____
Email/social media _____

Name _____ Number _____
Email/social media _____

Name _____ Number _____
Email/social media _____

Name _____ Number _____
Email/social media _____

Name _____ Number _____
Email/social media _____

Name _____ Number _____
Email/social media _____

Name _____ Number _____
Email/social media _____